I WAS PLAYING
CHECKERS
WHILE
GOD WAS PLAYING
CHESS

THE POWER AND PRESENCE
OF GOD IN MY LIFE

JAMES BASS

I Was Playing Checkers

While God was Playing Chess

The Power and Presence of God in My Life

By

James Bass

Published by Clarice Jefferies Publishing

Contact info: cjpublishing@yahoo.com

Copyright © 2025 James Bass

All rights reserved

For permissions, contact:

cjpublishing@yahoo.com

Printed in the United States of America on responsibly sourced paper.

CLARICE JEFFERIES

PASTOR EDWARD COLEMAN
PASTOR MARK SORONDO

Thank You

TABLE OF CONTENTS

INTRODUCTION

I used to think life was simple. A series of random moves—reactive, survival-driven.

I was playing checkers, hopping from one hardship to the next, just trying to stay in the game. But all along, **God was playing chess**. Every heartbreak, every betrayal, every unexpected blessing—none of it was random. Every piece was part of a divine strategy, a deliberate and loving orchestration I couldn't see at the time.

For most of my life, I didn't recognize the pattern. I questioned God. I doubted His presence. I raged against the brokenness of my life—abandoned, abused, shattered—and asked why I was even still standing. But now I see.

Every pain had a purpose. Every unanswered question was part of a greater plan.

This book isn't just my story. It's a **testimony**—a living reminder that while I was reacting to life, God was orchestrating something far bigger. I've wrestled with the questions most of us ask at some point:

If God is good, why does He allow suffering? Why do good people endure such pain? Why doesn't He step in sooner?

These aren't new questions. Job asked them. David cried them out in Psalms.

Even Jesus, on the cross, cried, *"My God, My God, why have You forsaken Me?"*

And yet, the answers aren't always what we expect.

First, **we live in a fallen world**—broken from the beginning by sin and marked by suffering, injustice, and death. Pain wasn't part of the original design but has become part of the human condition.

Still, God never promised to remove us from the suffering. **He promised to be with us through it.** Suffering refines us. It strips away illusions and draws us closer to the heart of God. Through pain, we develop compassion, resilience, faith, and perseverance.

Jesus Himself—the only truly innocent One—suffered brutally, not because God abandoned Him, but because there was a greater plan: **redemption**.

I spent years believing life was about fairness, good being rewarded, and bad being immediately punished. But if that were true, none of us would stand. Because who among us hasn't fallen short? Who among us is truly "good" all the time?

Jesus came not to deal out punishment but to offer **grace**. That's the thread running through every hardship in my life:

Not punishment—**preparation**.

Not abandonment—**alignment**.

I'm not a polished theologian. I'm not someone who shouts scripture from rooftops. My relationship with God has been like a lifelong conversation with an old, faithful friend— sometimes distant, sometimes desperate, but always real.

One Sunday at church, my Pastor preached a message that pierced me:

"We Are the Result of a Family Member's Prayers."

It was a revelation. Somewhere, someone in my bloodline had prayed for me. Maybe someone I never met, maybe someone who faced their own storms. But their prayers— those whispered cries to heaven—paved a path for me.

It wasn't luck that kept me alive. It wasn't coincidence that placed Abuela in my life. It wasn't chance that brought Crystal back to me after decades. It was God—making moves I couldn't see, crafting a strategy for my life with loving precision.

I realized that my story wasn't just a story of survival. It was the fulfillment of generations of prayers. It was the unfolding of moves God had planned before I ever took my first breath.

I used to attribute every good thing to luck. *I got lucky. You got lucky.* But after a while, the "coincidences" piled too high to ignore. Doors opened at just the right time. People appeared when I needed them most. Opportunities I wasn't qualified for fell into my lap. At some point, you have to stop calling it luck.

At some point, you have to recognize the hand of God.

My perspective changed when I finally stopped blaming luck and started recognizing divine alignment.

My past wasn't random…

My suffering wasn't wasted…

My blessings weren't accidental…

Every piece had been moved with purpose by a God who sees the entire board.

If you've ever felt abandoned, unseen, or stuck asking, "Why me?"—this book is for you.

If you've ever wondered if there's any meaning in the pain you carry—this book is for you.

If you've struggled to believe that your life matters or that your broken pieces could somehow be part of a bigger picture—this book is your reminder:

God is still moving. Even when you can't see it. You don't have to understand every move. You just have to trust the Master Player. It took me over four decades to finally realize:

God is in control. He was never reacting. He was always orchestrating. He was always thinking ahead, weaving my life into something bigger than I could comprehend.

This book is my story. But even more, it's a testimony to the God who never stopped moving—even when I did. I pray that as you turn these pages, you'll see your life differently, too. You'll see the patterns. The divine fingerprints. The perfect, loving moves.

Because **He's been playing chess with your life, too**. And the endgame is not defeat. It's **victory**.

I

THE FORK

The first chess move occurred long before I ever took my first breath. The journey to becoming the man I am today began 97 years ago, on January 20, 1927, in the vibrant city of Guadalajara, Mexico. God placed a queen onto the chessboard of my life—my Abuelita, Esperanza Armas. She would become more than just a grandmother. She would be my protector, my teacher, my spiritual compass—the first divine move that would one day save my life.

From the beginning, my abuela's existence was no accident. Her life was a sacred strategy. Long before I needed her, God prepared her to be a refuge in my coming storms.

By 1978, when I was just four years old, I was already drowning in chaos. Life with my biological mother was a constant storm of anger, resentment, and abuse. Her rage toward my absent father—an African American man who disappeared before I could even remember him—bled into her treatment of me. My dark skin was a daily reminder of a life she hated. Two stepfathers, who happened to be brothers, joined her in the cruelty.

From the age of four to seventeen, I endured emotional, physical, and mental abuse that left scars far deeper than anything visible. I lived under a heavy blanket of fear, shame, and survival. Home wasn't safe; it was a battlefield where my very existence seemed like a crime.

But then, there was my Abuelita.

When I crossed the threshold of her home, it felt like stepping into another universe—a place where love wasn't earned but given. She didn't always know the full extent of what was happening behind closed doors, but her heart knew enough. Her presence soothed wounds even she couldn't see.

Abuela's house was a haven—a place where I could be a child, if only for a few stolen hours. Her love was unconditional, her prayers relentless, and her arms a shelter against the raging storm of my life.

Yet even those safe moments were threatened. My mother and stepfathers wielded Abuela's love like a weapon, warning me that if I ever revealed the abuse, I would be cut off from her forever. Their threats kept me silent but made my time with her even more precious. To me, Abuelita wasn't just family. She was survival.

One memory stands out clearer than the rest—etched into my soul like a scar and a blessing all at once. I had been punished again.

The rule was brutal and simple: sit in the corner with a book in your lap. You can only move when you finish the book and write a report about it. There was one catch: I couldn't read.

Though I went to school, learning there was impossible. My days were filled with racial slurs and physical fights. "Nigger" was a word I heard more than my own name. The taunts about my dark skin pushed me into constant brawls, and eventually, I grew to hate school altogether. Ditching class became survival, not rebellion. As a result, my reading skills never developed.

My parents knew it. They used it.

For months, I sat isolated in the corner, staring blankly at books I couldn't understand, punished for a failure I had no way of fixing.

One day, as I sat trapped in that silent prison, my Abuelita arrived unexpectedly.

"¿Qué pasa, mijo?" she asked gently, her voice thick with concern.

I stumbled through an explanation, a mixture of shame, fear, and brokenness pouring out of me. Her warm hand brushed my cheek, and for the first time that day, I felt human again.

She didn't say much then. But I saw the flash of fury in her eyes as she left my room. The fierce love that boiled over into an argument with my mother loud enough to shake the walls. Abuelita didn't win that fight. But a few weeks later, she returned—with something better.

She carried a massive, heavy brown box. When I opened it, my eyes widened. Inside was a complete set of the *Encyclopedia Britannica*. Thirty volumes of wonder. Thirty volumes of freedom. "If they're going to punish you with reading," she said, "then you're going to become the smartest kid at your school."

At first, I didn't understand her plan. The books were intimidating and foreign. But as I flipped through the glossy pages filled with colorful images, something inside me stirred: curiosity, a thirst for knowledge, and hope I hadn't felt in years.

I began sounding out words…

Struggling through sentences…

Deciphering meaning from chaos…

Slowly, painfully, stubbornly—I learned…

Those encyclopedias became my companions. My escape. My silent teachers. Each fact about science, space, history, and medicine built a new world inside me—a world where I wasn't powerless—a world where I could grow beyond my pain.

Her gift was more than books. It was **a key**. It unlocked the prison of illiteracy. It planted a seed of resilience. It taught me that knowledge could be a weapon against oppression, a sword against silence.

I didn't realize it then, but Abuelita wasn't just giving me a way out of a corner—she was preparing me for a future battle I couldn't yet see. One day, I would need to understand psychiatric evaluations, decipher medical language, and fiercely advocate for someone I loved more than life itself. Without her, without those books, I would have been unequipped.

That encyclopedia set wasn't random. It was **God's first strategic move** on the board of my life. Looking back now, I see it so clearly. While I was playing checkers—reacting, surviving, staying one move ahead—**God was playing chess.**

He saw the abuse…

He saw the abandonment…

And He placed a queen in my life—a queen who would love me through the darkness and plant seeds of strength I would harvest decades later.

The Master had a plan. And this was only the beginning.

II

THE PIN

God's second chess move came in 1964, ten years before I entered the world.

That year, He placed a powerful, precious piece onto the board—**Crystal**, the woman who would one day become my wife, my anchor, and the catalyst for my healing. Her life, like mine, began with suffering.

Crystal was born into a family marred by abuse, neglect, and betrayal. She came into a world where love should have been her birthright but instead was a battlefield. The very people meant to protect and cherish her became sources of pain and fear. Her earliest memories were not of lullabies and safe embraces but of survival—scratching for hope in a world that seemed determined to crush her spirit.

Looking back now, I marvel at the intricate ways God was weaving our lives together long before we ever met. Though we were born a decade apart—Crystal in 1964, me in 1974—our paths bore striking similarities. Both of us were the eldest children in our families. Both of us had a younger brother and a younger sister.

Both of us were left fatherless at birth—abandoned by African American fathers who disappeared into the void, leaving behind only questions and wounds.

And both of us were thrust into homes filled with hardship rather than security.

The environments we grew up in, the trauma we carried, and the loneliness we learned to navigate—it all ran parallel, like two separate rivers destined to merge into one powerful current. Yet, even in suffering, our hearts responded differently.

While I allowed my pain to harden me—transforming my heart into a fortress of anger and distrust—Crystal somehow fought her darkness with light.

Where bitterness took root in me, hope bloomed in her. Where I built walls, she built bridges. Where I saw enemies, she saw possibilities. Her heart, bruised but unbeaten, remained a **beacon of love and faith**. She clung fiercely to the belief that God had a plan, even when her world gave her every reason to doubt it.

That kind of resilience wasn't human. It was divine. Crystal's spirit was forged in the silence—those hollow spaces where love should have lived but didn't.

And somehow, instead of letting that silence define her, she filled it with faith.

Faith that one day, life could be different...

Faith that love was still real...

Faith that even broken people could be made whole...

I didn't know it then, but while I was still a boy learning to fear the world, God had already placed Crystal as **my future rescue**. Her resilience would one day become my redemption. Her faith would one day awaken mine. When we finally met, it wasn't a fairy tale. It wasn't love at first sight, wrapped up in neat, easy romance.

It was raw...

It was messy...

It was two fractured souls colliding, neither fully ready for the storm or the sanctification that would follow. Crystal saw something in me that I could not see in myself. While I was drowning in anger, mistrust, and self-destruction, she saw the man buried underneath the rubble—the man I was always meant to be. And her love wasn't passive. It wasn't weak. It was **God's strategy made into flesh**.

It would take years—and many wounds—for me to realize just how intentional her presence was in my life. But one conversation in 2007 became the turning point that shattered every wall I had ever built. During a bitter argument, frustrated and callous, I hurled a rhetorical question at her:

"If I'm such a horrible person, why are you still with me? Why do you still love me?"

Without hesitation, with tears in her eyes but steel in her voice, she answered:

"I love you not for the man you are. I love you for the man you will become."

Those words pierced through the darkness that had gripped my soul for decades.

They didn't excuse my brokenness. They didn't deny the pain I had caused.

But they **prophesied redemption**. Crystal didn't love me because of who I had been—she loved me because of **who God was still calling me to become**.

Her love saw beyond the present chaos into the divine potential God had planted within me. That was no accident. That was a **divine chess move**. Her unwavering faith in God and me became the chisel that cracked open my hardened heart. She showed me that love is not just a feeling—it's a force.

It's a catalyst...

It's a lifeline...

Through Crystal's relentless grace, I learned that **healing was possible**. That trust wasn't a fantasy. That love could be stronger than fear. And in that surrender, I realized something even greater: Crystal's birth wasn't a coincidence. Our matching scars weren't meaningless. Our suffering wasn't wasted. **It was God's design.**

Every hurt...

Every lonely night...

Every desperate prayer...

Every moment of resilience forged through pain...

It was all part of a greater story—a grand strategy penned by the Master Himself.

Crystal's life, her faith, her strength—**they weren't just for her**. They were a gift to me. A signpost pointing back to a God who never abandoned either of us, even when it felt like the whole world had.

Through Crystal, I learned to hope again. To believe again. To live again.

Because love—the real, reckless, divine kind—**doesn't just heal wounds.**

It resurrects dead hearts. And her love resurrected mine.

III

THE SKEWER

T he summer of 1983 marked God's third strategic move in the divine plan for my life. It unfolded not in a church or a grand miracle but in a place most would overlook: the Greyhound Bus Depot in downtown Fresno, California.

I was nine years old, lost in a world of chaos and confusion. My stepfather, Rock, worked long, grueling graveyard shifts at the depot as the shop foreman and lead mechanic. Every evening around 5:30, my mother would pack me and my younger siblings into the car, deliver his dinner, and, unknowingly, deliver me into a moment that would change the course of my life.

As my mother disappeared into the mechanics' bay, my brother and I wandered through the bustling terminal. The depot was alive with movement—people clutching their tickets, boarding buses bound for places I could only dream about. It felt like another world to a boy like me—a place of endless possibilities and unknown destinations.

We often found ourselves inside the Burger King tucked inside the depot, a small haven promising a burger, fries, and for my brother and me, the real treasure: an arcade.

While my brother raced to the flashing lights of the video games, I would drift toward the counter, dollar bills clutched tightly in my hand, waiting for my turn to exchange the dollars for quarters. And that's when my spirit saw her. Crystal.

She was eighteen then, a high school senior working behind the counter, dressed in her fast-food uniform, preparing meals for weary travelers.

I didn't know her name. We didn't speak. We didn't even lock eyes. But in my peripheral, I saw her. And somehow—without a word—something in me would **remember her**. Through my young eyes, still too innocent to understand the full weight of the moment, she wasn't just another teenager flipping burgers.

She was light.

Gentle...

Anchoring...

In a place filled with noise and strangers, Crystal's presence was a silent, sacred contrast—like a candle flickering quietly in a storm. It wasn't love at first sight. It wasn't attraction or fantasy.

It was **recognition**...

A stirring of something eternal...

Now, decades later, I see it for what it truly was. It was **divine choreography**.

It was **God's third move**—a moment quietly stamped onto the timeline of my soul, waiting for its complete revelation. At the time, I couldn't have known how much we shared. That Crystal's childhood was a mirror of my own - shattered by abandonment, bruised by betrayal.

That her heart, like mine, bore the scars of longing and the ache of survival.

Two broken spirits crossing paths for the first time—not to change each other yet, but to be *marked* for later. This was no coincidence. It was the **first glimpse of destiny**. A cosmic connection crafted by the Master Himself.

To understand moments like these, you must understand divine orchestration's nature. It's not loud. It's not obvious. It's subtle. Silent. Sacred.

We expect God's movements to be wrapped in signs and wonders. But more often, He moves quietly—like a Grandmaster positioning His pieces with infinite patience, setting up victories we won't recognize until much later. That night at the Greyhound Depot wasn't about romance. It was about **alignment**.

It was about **weaving threads**—two lives, separated by a decade, each battered by different storms, yet destined to intertwine in a tapestry far more beautiful than either could imagine. Our spirits brushed in that fleeting moment. And though neither of us understood it, Heaven smiled. Because a future was being written.

A future where Crystal's love would one day pierce through the violent darkness clouding my heart. A future where her unwavering hope would challenge my despair. A future where two broken kids would build a new legacy—one founded not on pain but grace.

We were two souls destined to meet. Two prayers—answered in advance. Two pieces on God's chessboard—moved precisely into position. Reflecting now, I realize that **divine connections are rarely understood in real-time**.

They are planted as seeds in the soil of ordinary days. They grow quietly, nurtured by tears, tests, and time. And then, when God is ready, they bloom into something we finally recognize as a miracle.

That summer evening, in the noisy chaos of a bus depot arcade, I unknowingly brushed against the future. And God, smiling behind the veil, whispered:

"I'm working. Even now. Even here."

This was not just a boy spotting a teenage girl. This was **destiny, glancing across the room**. The third move had been made. The board was set. And the game—the beautiful, redemptive, God-ordained game—was beginning.

IV
DISCOVERED ATTACK

Nine years would pass since that fleeting glimpse at the Greyhound Bus Depot.

Nine years since I, a wide-eyed boy, caught sight of a radiant spirit behind a Burger King counter—a spirit mine would never forget.

And now, in the summer of 1992, God's fourth move in His divine plan unfolded.

I was eighteen, working as an assistant lifeguard at Frank H. Playground on the west side of Fresno. My aunt, a close friend of the playground's manager, had helped me get the job. For the first time in a long while, I found a small sense of belonging.

The playground was my sanctuary—a place where responsibility anchored me when everything else still felt uncertain. When I wasn't watching over the pool, I worked in the small office, taking admission fees.

Most days blurred together—children laughing, splashing water, the hum of life moving forward. But one boy stood out. He came daily with a group of friends yet never swam. He was always on the sidelines, a silent observer. One sweltering afternoon, I asked him why. With his head lowered and his voice soft, he said, "My mom forgot to give me money."

Something inside me broke. I knew that feeling all too well—the sting of being left out because of things beyond your control. Without a second thought, I pulled out a few dollars and paid for him. That day. And the next. And the next. Lunches, too, when I could. Not out of obligation—but because kindness had once been my only lifeline too.

Day after day, we shared those small moments—laughter over hamburgers, jokes over juice boxes. They were brief, but they mattered. Then, one day, he was gone.

No warning. No goodbye. I missed him more than I expected.

But life moved on, and I continued showing up, unaware that God was positioning the next significant piece on my board. About a month later, it happened.

She walked into the building...

Crystal.

The high school girl from the Burger King counter. Not the nameless memory tucked away in the depth of my subconscious. But Crystal—flesh and blood, light and strength, standing just a few feet away from me.

She spoke with another employee first, asking for "James." When they pointed her toward me, I felt a jolt deep in my chest—a stirring I couldn't explain, a feeling that whispered: *Home.*

She introduced herself, thanking me for looking after her nephew. Her eyes, filled with gratitude, were locked with mine. And in that instant, I knew.

It wasn't about the pool...

It wasn't about the boy...

It was about *this*—the divine moment when two souls, long connected by invisible threads, finally found each other again. There was a familiarity in her gaze—a silent understanding. Not recognition of a face, but recognition of a spirit.

A soul I had seen before. A soul God had chosen for me.

It wasn't coincidence...

It wasn't luck...

It was **divine alignment**...

The kindness I had shown her nephew wasn't just an act of compassion—it was a chess move orchestrated by a Master who saw the whole board. Each dollar spent, each Frito boat shared, and each laugh was part of the plan to bring us back together.

And though we didn't start dating immediately, something eternal was set in motion that day. As I reflect on it now, I see it with complete clarity:

God was never just reuniting two people...

He was reuniting two survivors...

Two warriors...

He had been healing two broken hearts in parallel, preparing them to be part of something far greater than either could have imagined alone. We weren't just meeting for romance. We were meeting for *the mission.*

To heal...

To fight for each other...

To break generational curses together...

Crystal's return wasn't the beginning of a love story. It was the next precise move in **a divine mission**—a mission written by the hand of a God who sees every tear, every scar, every hidden dream and still says, *"Wait. I'm not finished yet."*

That summer marked not just a reconnection. It marked the beginning of destiny unfolding. A thread once planted in the quiet of a bus depot is now woven tightly around our lives. God had made His move. And once again, the board shifted forever.

V

DISCOVERED CHECK

More than a decade would pass since Crystal and I first reconnected. In 2005, we stood at the altar, two survivors ready to start a new life together. Our union was sealed not just with vows but also with the belief that love could heal even the deepest wounds. But love, alone, doesn't erase scars...

Beneath the surface of our new beginning, a storm raged within me.

Years of unhealed trauma. Years of abandonment, cruelty, and violence were embedded into my very bones. I carried those shadows into our marriage like silent weapons. And all too often, I wielded them against the one person who loved me the most.

I was unfaithful…

I was angry…

I was violent…

Not because I didn't love Crystal—but because I didn't know how to love myself.

My mother's voice still echoed in my mind:

"You're a sorry ass nigger like your father."

"You're stupid."

"You should have been aborted."

Her hatred had carved deep grooves into my soul, grooves that no amount of new beginnings could simply fill. I cheated—not for lust, but for validation. I chased fleeting moments of feeling "wanted," trying to fill a bottomless void left by a mother who could never love me the way I needed.

I drank to silence the demons…I smoked weed to numb the pain…

I fought—at work, on the streets, anywhere rage could find an outlet. I lashed out—verbally, mentally, even physically—at Crystal, the one person who stood between me and complete self-destruction.

My life became a war zone, and Crystal was caught in the crossfire. She bore my rage, my guilt, my shame—all while continuing to love me in a way I couldn't comprehend. And worst of all?

I hated myself for it...

I hated that I couldn't control it...

I hated becoming the very monster I had vowed never to be...

Each drink, each fight, and each betrayal drove me deeper into despair.

Externally, I wore the mask of a formidable man—feared, respected, and even admired for my strength. But inside, I was losing a battle I didn't know how to fight.

I remember one night vividly lying next to Crystal, her breathing soft and even, while guilt suffocated me. I had just returned from being with another woman.

I stared at the ceiling, feeling like a fraud, aching to wake her up and confess everything—yet paralyzed by fear that if I spoke the truth, the only real love I had ever known would forever disappear. And maybe part of me thought I deserved to lose her. Yet somehow, despite it all, Crystal stayed.

Not mindlessly...

Not naively...

But because God had equipped her with a love **stronger than my brokenness**. And then came the night everything changed. It was June 2007. We had fought—again.

My cruel words...

Heavy silences...

Her tears...

Crystal lay crumpled on the carpet, sobbing. I stood over her, hollow and broken, unable to face what I had become. From the depths of my cowardice, I threw a bitter, defensive question into the room:

"If I'm such a horrible person, why are you still with me? Why do you still love me?"

Through her tears, Crystal looked up at me with a strength that shook the foundations of my soul. And she answered: **"I don't love you for the man you are. I love you for the man you're going to become."** And in that moment—I heard it.

Check...

God had made His move. That sentence, spoken through Crystal's trembling voice, was a divine strike against every lie I had ever believed about myself. It wasn't just love.

It was prophecy...

It was warfare...

It was God reaching into the deepest, most broken place inside me and declaring:

"You are not beyond redemption."

Something inside me shattered that night.

Not Crystal...

Not our marriage...

Me...

The old James—the man ruled by rage, shame, and generational curses—began to die. And the man God had always seen—the man Crystal had always believed in—began to breathe for the first time. It wasn't instant. Transformation rarely is.

But that night was my turning point.

That night, the board shifted forever. Crystal's love wasn't just endurance. It was divine alignment. It was God positioning her—not merely to comfort me—but to **call me into my destiny**. Her faith in my future sparked a war inside me.

A war between who I had been... and who I was still called to become.

And though it took time—through countless battles with addiction, anger, and shame—I chose to fight.

I chose to believe her...

I chose to believe Him...

Because God's move wasn't to destroy me. It was to **check** me—to halt my spiral, to force a decision, to remind me that even broken kings can be restored. Crystal's words became my compass. Her tears became my altar. Her unwavering love became the echo of God's voice, whispering: *"You are not done yet."*

The fifth move was made. The board was set. And by God's grace, the next move was mine to make.

VI
DOUBLE CHECK

A fter that night in June 2007, when Crystal's words cracked me open, something inside me began to change. For the first time in my life, I stopped long enough to see my life for what it truly was: A game I didn't understand, a game I had never played with purpose.

I had been living like a man stuck in a game of checkers—hopping from square to square, reacting to whatever life threw at me.

Quick moves...

Short-term survival...

No strategy...

No vision beyond the next crisis...

While God had been orchestrating moves with eternity in mind, I had been trying simply to stay afloat.

React...

Retreat...

Survive...

But **God wasn't playing checkers.** He was playing **chess**. Every move in my life—the abuse, the abandonment, the glimpses of love, the betrayals, the gifts, even the unbearable pain—had been **intentional**.

Every heartbreak carried a lesson...

Every delay was filled with divine timing...

I finally began to understand, **I wasn't being punished. I was being prepared.**

That summer, I sat alone at work, reflecting. For the first time in years, I could hear God speaking—not in loud declarations, but in clarity, in the gentle pressing against my spirit.

"Son, I didn't bring you this far just to have you jump from one square to the next," He whispered. *"It's time to live with intention."*

And so, I did something simple, something sacred: **I stopped blaming.**

I stopped blaming my mother...

I stopped blaming my absent father...

I stopped blaming the world...

I even stopped blaming God...

I realized I was no longer the powerless child trapped by circumstance. I was a man—with a full board of pieces, waiting to be moved with strategy, vision, and purpose. My healing began with **accountability**. And with Crystal by my side—patient, persistent, and full of grace—I began to lay down the checker pieces.

I started to think before reacting...

To plan before leaping...

To build instead of merely surviving...

For so long, I believed survival was the best I could hope for. But now I knew **thriving** was what God had intended for me all along. It wasn't just about changing behavior. It was about **changing perspective**.

I had to start seeing my life through the eyes of a Master Strategist—One who didn't waste a single move, a single tear, a single scar. Crystal had been playing chess long before I realized another game was being played.

Despite her traumas, she moved through life with purpose, direction, and hope.

Watching her inspired me to believe that I could live that way too. Her resilience showed me that pain didn't have to define me. It could refine me.

Sitting at work one afternoon, I made a silent vow: I would no longer settle for reactionary living. I would learn to play chess.

I wanted more than survival...

I wanted strategy...

I wanted vision...

I wanted a life shaped not by fear of the next blow but by faith in the ultimate victory already secured for me. From that moment on, everything shifted.

Each choice I made, each step I took, was now part of a larger picture—a picture I couldn't yet fully see but trusted God was painting.

The checkerboard I had known—the quick, anxious scramble for survival—was gone. Now, I was standing before a chessboard. The pieces were set. The plan was unfolding. And for the first time in my life, I realized: **It was my move.**

VII
ZWISCHENZUG

D espite the miracles and moments of grace that had already marked my life, my faith still staggered. I believed in God, yes. But **trust**—that radical, unshakable trust that can survive trauma, silence, and unanswered prayers—that was something I hadn't yet fully learned.

Then came the night that shattered every illusion I had about control. The night Crystal disappeared. We had faced the battles of psychosis before—terrifying delusions, hallucinations, the relentless war within her mind. But this time was different. This time, it wasn't just in her head. This time, it was physical. This time, she was gone.

No wallet...

No plan...

No right of mind...

Just gone— broken, and alone somewhere in the vast city streets. And I broke. Hours of searching. Hours of pleading. Hours of bargaining and begging. Hospitals had no record of her. Police officers treated me more like a suspect than a desperate husband.

Every scenario that played in my mind ended in tragedy. I cried out to God with the kind of desperation that strips a man to his bones. But while I was unraveling, God was making His final, undeniable move.

Earlier that day, Crystal had suffered one of the worst psychotic breaks I had ever witnessed. In her mind, I had become her childhood abuser—the man who had once shattered her innocence. In her terror, she opened the car door, attempting to escape into oncoming traffic.

I had no choice but to wrestle her back to safety, holding her tightly against her will—protecting her even as she fought me like a wounded animal. The woman I loved, the woman who had saved me with her words and her faith, now saw me as the enemy.

It was heartbreaking beyond words. When the paramedics and police arrived, I thought relief would come. Instead, I was met with suspicion. They didn't see the frantic husband trying to save his wife. They saw another man capable of harm.

Despite my warnings and my desperate explanations, they restrained Crystal under a 51/50 hold and took her away.

At least she would be safe, I thought...

At least she would be monitored, stabilized, and cared for...

But when I arrived at the hospital to check on her, ready to sit by her side for however long it took, the receptionist frowned and said words that sent ice through my veins: **"We have no patient by that name."**

At first, I thought it was a clerical mistake. A misspelled name. A transfer to another facility. But the truth was far worse. Despite the mandatory 72-hour psychiatric hold, the hospital had allowed Crystal to walk out—alone, disoriented, still gripped by psychosis.

Crystal was missing. Again. And this time, no one had any idea where to begin looking. I filed a missing person's report. I called hospitals, shelters—anywhere someone confused and barefoot might have ended up.

And after it all, I prayed like I had never prayed before:

"Please, God. Please watch over her. Please keep her safe. Please bring her back to me."

Hours blurred into agony. I pictured every terrible possibility—Crystal wandering into traffic, Crystal falling victim to the elements, Crystal hurt, scared, dying. I was powerless. But I wasn't alone. Somewhere deep inside, despite my fear, a thread of faith held on.

Not perfect faith...

Not unshakable faith...

But faith forged in desperation, crying out to a God who had always been playing a better game than I could see. And then—seventeen hours after she vanished—Crystal came stumbling up our driveway.

Barefoot...

Bruised...

Dehydrated...

Still wearing her hospital scrubs...

Her feet were bruised and swollen from miles of wandering. But alive. She had walked over twelve miles in a severe state of psychosis—across freeways, intersections, and dangerous neighborhoods—guided by nothing but the unseen hand of God.

She didn't know where she was going.... But God did. That moment wasn't luck.

It wasn't a coincidence...

It was **checkmate**...

Not the end of the game. But the undeniable victory of a Master who had never left the board. I stood there, overcome with gratitude and awe, realizing a truth I could no longer deny: **God never lost control.**

He never lost control when I doubted...

He never lost control when I cursed Him...

He never lost control when fear told me all hope was gone...

While I scrambled in panic, God had already secured the outcome. He had not abandoned us in our suffering. He had been guiding every step—even the bloodied, broken ones.

In a game of chess, checkmate is the objective, it is the ultimate triumph. It not only signals the end of the game but the culmination of calculated moves that lead to the victory. And in that moment, I knew beyond a shadow of a doubt:

The King was still on His throne.

Crystal's survival was a miracle—a declaration that God's plans are never defeated by human fear or brokenness.

He had seen every move...

He had prepared every defense...

He had led her back, footstep by painful footstep, to the place where His promises would be fulfilled. The battle wasn't over. But the war for my faith had been won.

From that night forward, my trust in God was no longer built on theory.

It was built on living, breathing, undeniable **grace**. And I finally understood...

In God's game, the King always wins.

VIII
THE SACRIFICE

W hen I finally accepted that God had been orchestrating this game all along, I knew it was time for me to start playing, too—not with fear or survival instincts but with **faith** and **strategy**. It started with assembling the pieces.

The life experiences that once seemed random and cruel— the abuse I survived, the isolation, my abuela's steadfast love, Crystal's patience, the battles, the heartbreaks—all of it had been intentional.

Not punishments...

Preparations...

Now, it was up to me to use what God had given me. Crystal's return after her disappearance didn't mean the storm was over.

Far from it. Her mental health journey was an ongoing battle, a cycle of unpredictable spirals, hospitalizations, medications, and moments of pure helplessness.

There were days when the shadows of her past would overtake her completely, days when even I became a stranger in her mind. But I wasn't the same man anymore. I was no longer reacting like a child trapped in survival mode. I was learning to anticipate, to prepare, to stand with strategy—like a grandmaster guarding something sacred.

I realized that God hadn't just been shaping me to survive my past. He had been training me to **protect** Crystal's future. I became her advocate. Her voice when she couldn't speak for herself. Her shield when her mind turned against her.

I studied her diagnosis like a man who studies a foreign language, desperate to communicate love through understanding. I researched medications, side effects, and therapy   techniques.

I sat through doctor's appointments with a notebook in hand, asking the questions others didn't think to ask. I fought with insurance companies, with hospitals, with anyone who treated her like a file number instead of a human soul. And every time I cracked open a medical journal, every time I deciphered confusing psychiatric terminology, I remembered the brown box my abuela gave me when I was just a broken boy sitting in a corner.

The box filled with encyclopedias...

The box that sparked my hunger to learn...

It hadn't been random...

It had been **training**...

God had seen decades ahead, knowing there would come a time when I would need that hunger—not for grades or achievement—but to save the woman who would one day save me.

Each piece of my past—each punishment, each heartbreak, each unanswered prayer—had been forming the man Crystal would one day need. And now, I could finally see the board clearly. This wasn't just about our marriage. This wasn't just about surviving another psychotic break or another hospital stay.

This was about **purpose**...

Purpose begins the moment you stop playing defense and start moving with **vision**. It was time to live, love, and fight with intention.

So, I moved...

I chose to stay...

I chose to build...

I chose to believe that our scars weren't signs of defeat—they were **testimonies of survival**. I stopped seeing myself as a victim of life's chaos. I stopped seeing Crystal as broken beyond repair.

Instead, I started to see us as **part of a divine strategy**—a plan unfolding with every tear, every prayer, every small, stubborn act of love. On the chessboard of our life together, I wasn't just a pawn anymore.

I was her knight, standing between her and the darkness...

I was her bishop, guiding her through the fog of confusion...

I was her rook, a solid fortress when everything else felt unstable...

And above all, I was a man who finally understood:

God had already secured the victory.

Our role was to trust Him and move with purpose. Life isn't about avoiding battles. It's about assembling your pieces, trusting your King, and stepping into the fight knowing the outcome has already been written.

Crystal's journey isn't over. There are still hard days, still nights filled with prayers and waiting. But now, I know the truth:

Every move matters...

Every piece has a purpose...

And no matter how chaotic the board looks—**the Master never loses.**

IX

BACK RANK MATE

When Crystal's illness deepened into a darkness few could fathom—hallucinations, paranoia, delusions—I found myself in unfamiliar, terrifying territory. I wasn't just her husband anymore.

I became her lifeline...

Her caretaker...

Her protector...

Her voice when hers was lost to the chaos...

At first, I was overwhelmed. There's no manual for loving someone through psychosis. There are no easy answers when the person you love looks at you with fear instead of recognition. I didn't know how to help someone whose reality was fractured by unseen terrors. I didn't speak the language of her pain.

I often felt like I was standing helplessly on the shore, watching her drown in a storm I couldn't stop. But God had already made provisions. His earlier moves—my abuela's love, her gift of knowledge, and the resilience forged in childhood suffering—had all prepared me for this moment.

I remembered how my abuela loved me through the darkest, most humiliating days of my life.

She didn't love me because I was easy to love...

She didn't love me because I earned it...

She loved me because love, in its purest form, **is unconditional**. Her hands were gentle when the world was brutal. Her voice was steady when the world was filled with hate. It was that love that saved me then. And it was that love God now called me to give to Crystal. That realization broke me open in the best way.

I stopped trying to "fix" Crystal...

I stopped trying to get "my wife back..."

I stopped grieving what was lost...

Instead, I started **showing up**...

I chose to love her as she was, in whatever mental state she was in. Some days, she didn't recognize me. Some days, she was terrified of me. Other days, she clung to me like I was her only tether to reality. But through it all, I stood firm.

Not because it was easy...

Not because it was fair...

But because it was **divine**...

God wasn't asking me to endure Crystal's illness. He was inviting me to **fight for her** with the most potent weapon He had ever given me: **Unconditional love.**

It wasn't a weakness...

It wasn't unquestioning loyalty...

It was warfare...

Every time, I held Crystal's hand in a psychiatric hospital room. Every time, I whispered her name through the fog of her delusions. Every time I stayed, when fear and exhaustion whispered that it would be easier to leave— I was waging a war against the darkness that sought to swallow her whole. And something unexpected happened.

In loving Crystal through her brokenness, I began to feel **my own healing take root**. The love I had received from my abuela all those years ago—steady, stubborn, unconditional— was now flowing through me. It wasn't just helping Crystal survive. It was **transforming me**.

Each moment of fear...

Each hospital visit...

Each whispered prayer at her bedside...

It became an altar where God reshaped my heart. He showed me that true love isn't about ease or comfort. It's about **choosing**—again and again—to stay, to fight, to believe when everything around you tells you to give up.

It's about being a shelter when someone's mind becomes a battlefield. It's about being a voice of peace when fear screams louder than anything else. And it's about realizing that love's true power isn't proven in the good times. It's proven in the trenches.

My abuela's legacy—the seed of unconditional love she planted in my heart decades earlier—was now blooming in the most unlikely soil. And Crystal's unwavering love for me, even through my darkest seasons, had prepared the ground.

As I stood by Crystal, day after day, I felt God's presence so near it was almost tangible. A whisper on the winds of chaos:

"This is what real love looks like. This kind of love changes the world—one soul at a time."

Loving Crystal wasn't just about saving her. It was about saving me, too.

It was about redeeming the broken boy who once sat alone in a corner, unloved and unseen. It was about proving that love, in its purest form, is the most powerful, most holy force in the universe.

And as I looked into her eyes—whether they were clear or clouded—I knew:

This love was not mine. It was God's. And it was enough.

X
CLEARANCE SACRIFICE

February 2020 was a turning point. Crystal had been hospitalized again, trapped inside another spiral of confusion and fear, and I stood at a crossroad no husband ever imagines standing at:

Do I leave her in the care of professionals?

Or do I bring her home under my own care, trusting in nothing but the preparation God has given me?

I had no medical degree...

No formal clinical training...

No credentials anyone would recognize...

Just a battered heart, years of observation, and a mind sharpened by a childhood no one would envy. In those moments of fear and uncertainty, God reminded me of something small but sacred, the encyclopedia set my abuela had given me as a boy.

What once felt like punishment—those endless hours of struggling to read, wrestling with knowledge that seemed out of reach—wasn't punishment.

It was **preparation**...

Those dusty books taught me how to consume complex information and decode the mysteries of the world through patience, perseverance, and faith. And now, that same skill was being called into battle. So, I moved. I bought a copy of the DSM-5—the diagnostic and statistical manual of mental disorders used by doctors and clinicians worldwide.

Its pages were thick with jargon and dense with complicated terminology.

But I wasn't afraid. Because deep inside, that little boy who once fought to sound out words had become a man capable of decoding the language of healing.

I dove headfirst into research...

I devoured psychiatric journals...

I studied Crystal's medications—how they worked, their side effects, and their interactions. I enrolled in Harvard Medical School's online courses, deepening my understanding with rigorous studies late into the night.

My home became a classroom...

My notebook became a lifeline...

And I—mechanic/commercial driver by trade, husband by love, student by divine appointment—became both nurse and neurologist, protector and priest.

Every time I studied a new chapter, every time I journaled a shift in her behavior, every time I caught a side effect before it became a crisis, I could hear the quiet voice of God whisper:

"See? You thought you were being punished.

But I was preparing you all along."

Finally, the decision became clear. I discharged Crystal. Not because I distrusted doctors. Not because I thought I was better. But because I finally trusted **God's preparation**.

I realized that no clinician, no psychiatrist, no system knew her the way I did.

No one else could see the tiny, almost invisible shifts in her mood.

No one else loved her enough to treat her as a soul, not just a case number. Crystal didn't need just medication...

She needed **tenderness**...

She needed **presence**...

She needed someone who would fight not just for her survival but for her dignity.

Discharging her wasn't an act of pride. It was an act of **stewardship**.

God had entrusted her to me. And now He was empowering me to lead—not out of expertise, but out of empathy. And so, I led. I monitored her progress meticulously. I advocated fiercely when something didn't feel right. I adjusted routines, medications, and treatments with careful precision, always praying and listening for the quiet nudges of the Holy Spirit. And she improved.

Slowly...

Painfully...

Miraculously...

Every small step of healing was another confirmation that God hadn't wasted a single moment of my life.

Not the beatings...

Not the brokenness...

Not the hours spent alone with encyclopedias no one thought I would ever understand. **Every piece had a purpose. Every move had been part of His plan.**

Looking back, I realize now that purpose isn't something we stumble into by accident. It's built—piece by piece—through the trials we survive, the lessons we endure, the knowledge we gather, and the love we choose to give even when it costs everything.

When I sat as a boy in a corner, struggling to read, it felt like punishment.

When I stood as a man beside Crystal's hospital bed, it felt like destiny.

Because the truth is this: **God had been preparing me all along.**

Not just to survive...

But to heal...

To lead...

To love with the fierce, informed, relentless passion of a man who finally understood his assignment. The chessboard was clear now. The next move was mine. And this time, I would move with intention, knowing that every step forward was part of a divine strategy far greater than anything I could have imagined.

DECOY

There's a strange silence after a storm—a stillness that invites reflection.

After everything Crystal and I had endured—her battles with psychosis, my battles with my past, our long nights of healing—I found myself holding something unexpected...

A pen.

Crystal had seen it long before I ever did. Years earlier, after I stood toe-to-toe with a powerful corporate attorney at an unemployment hearing—armed with nothing but truth and determination—and won, she told me something I never forgot.

"You need to write," she said. *"Your voice matters."*

At the time, I laughed it off. **Me?** Write a book? But now, standing on the other side of battles that had nearly broken us, something shifted.

After Crystal came home from the hospital in 2020, as I documented every detail of her recovery, my notebooks started looking less like medical logs and more like a story. **Our story.**

And slowly, the voice I thought had been beaten out of me as a boy—the voice silenced by years of abuse and fear—began to return. I remembered the lies my mother drilled into me: *"You'll never amount to anything. You're going to be nothing but a sorry ass nigger just like your father."*

But now, I had proof she was wrong...

Because in my pain, I found **purpose**...

And in my story, I found **power**...

Late at night, while Crystal slept, I wrote. Between outpatient visits and medication adjustments, I scribbled. At first, it was raw. Jagged. Messy. But it was **real**. I wasn't just writing about symptoms. I was writing about survival. About love.

About God's relentless pursuit of broken people. And then came the memory—the first seed Crystal had planted over two decades earlier during one of the most challenging seasons of my life.

I had spent almost a decade working for an employer where racism, discrimination, and hostility were my daily companions. Eventually, after years of enduring abuse, I was let go. Facing a powerful corporate attorney in an unemployment hearing was supposed to be an unwinnable battle. But I stood my ground.

I told my truth...

And I won...

Crystal, standing proudly beside me, said it again: *"You need to write. Your voice can help people."*

Back then, I couldn't see it. Back then, my mother's words still echoed too loudly in my mind. Back then, I was still shackled by shame, believing I was nothing more than the broken boy she said I would always be.

But now???

Now, with a heart full of battles won and a pen full of truth, I could finally see:

Crystal hadn't just seen my potential. She had been **prophesying** over my life.

So, I kept writing.

I wrote through exhaustion...

I wrote through tears...

I wrote through doubt, fear, and the whispers of old lies that told me no one would care.

In October 2022, my autobiography, **In Love with My 5 Wives: A Broken Man's Journey on How to Love His Broken Wife**, was published.

Released on Amazon, it quickly became the #1 New Release in five categories: **Medicine and Psychology**, **Medical Mental Illness**, **Marriage**, **Schizophrenia**, and **Dissociative Disorders**.

In 2024, it was honored with multiple awards:

- ☐ The **Literary Titan Gold Award**

- ☐ The **PenCraft Excellence in Writing Award**

- ☐ The **PenCraft Best Book of the Summer Award**

The response was overwhelming, so in 2024, I decided to write a follow up titled, **Back to Loving My 1st Wife: A Husband's Unconditional Love & The Aftermath of Caregiver Stress.**

In 2024, it was honored with multiple awards:

- ☐ The **Literary Titan Gold Award**

- ☐ The **International Impact Book Award**

- ☐ Nomination for **2025 International Impact Author of The Year**

Awards I humbly give back to the One who made all this possible...

Not to impress...

Not to perform...

But to proclaim that **healing is real**, that **God doesn't waste pain**, and that **broken people still have beautiful,**

powerful purposes. The exact words that once cursed me became the ink that freed others. And what began with a brown box of encyclopedias, handed to a boy only my Abuelita believed in, became a testimony that no suffering is wasted in the hands of God.

And now, with Crystal by my side, my pen in my hand, and my heart firmly rooted in God's faithfulness, I understand:

This is not just **my story**. It's **His masterpiece**.

ZUGZWANG

If writing helped me find my voice, speaking helped me give it away. The first time I stood in front of a crowd to share my story, my knees trembled. My palms were sweaty. Fear gnawed at my heart.

What if they judge me?

What if they don't understand?

What if my story isn't enough?

But then I spoke—and something holy happened. People nodded. People cried.

People prayed. And I knew:

This wasn't about me...

It wasn't about impressing anyone...

It wasn't about performing perfection...

It was about the single mother battling depression in silence...

It was about the husband trying to help a wife he no longer recognized...

It was about the person with an addiction hiding shame...

It was about the survivor wondering if they could ever feel whole again...

It was about every broken soul who has ever looked up to the heavens and whispered: **"Why me?"**

Every speaking engagement became a pulpit—not of polished faith, but of genuine faith. The kind that clings to God when everything hurts. The kind that doesn't offer easy answers but simply offers presence and hope. I stopped being a prisoner of my past. I became a witness to **God's power**.

I shared about trauma...

About marriage...

About forgiveness...

About identity...

I didn't speak from the polished podium of a therapist. I spoke from the bloodied battlefield I knew too well. And with every testimony, I felt God smiling.

Because His plan for me wasn't survival.

It was **light**.

This move—**stepping into the light**—was about legacy. It was about turning every breakdown into a breakthrough.

Every loss into a lesson...

Every scar into a story of redemption...

And if God could redeem my broken life, then He could redeem **anyone's**.

It wasn't easy at first. Vulnerability never is. Writing my book had been a shield—I could edit, polish, hide behind pages. But speaking?

Speaking was raw...

Unfiltered...

It demanded courage I wasn't sure I had. I was terrified the first time I shared openly about Crystal's mental health battles, about my struggles with rage, depression, and self-doubt. The words caught in my throat. But as I looked into the faces of the audience—men and women, young and old—I saw something miraculous:

Recognition...

Pain mirrored in their eyes...

Tears of silent battles they had been too afraid to name...

And that's when I realized something critical: **Vulnerability doesn't weaken us. It frees us.**

By exposing my wounds, I was allowing them to heal. And I was giving others permission to start healing, too. Men who had never spoken a word about their pain came up to me afterward, whispering their confessions, their fears, their desperate hopes. I was no longer just telling my story.

I was helping unlock theirs.

We live in a world where men are told to be strong, silent, and untouchable.

Where struggle is weakness and emotion is failure. But that's a lie straight from hell. The truth is:

Real strength is being honest about your battles...

Real courage is choosing to heal...

I never thought this would be my path. But now that I'm on it, I can't imagine doing anything else. Every time I approach a microphone, every time I open my heart and let the words fall out, I remember why I do this:

I do it for the man drowning in silence...

I do it for the couple clinging to love in the middle of mental health battles...

I do it for the little boy still hiding in the corner of his mind, waiting to be seen and loved.

And I do it for the God who never gave up on me—even when I gave up on myself.

This journey has taught me something I'll carry forever:

Purpose isn't something you find. It's something you create—through God's divine plan, through surrender, through survival, and through courage.

Healing isn't a one-time victory—it's a lifelong battle. But every time we speak, every time we share, every time we choose love over silence—**We win another battle.**

So, if you're reading this today and you're struggling, know this…You are not alone.

It's okay to be vulnerable…

It's okay to ask for help…

It's okay to fight for your happiness and healing…

Your story matters and when you share it—You don't just heal yourself. You help heal others, too.

XIII

THE BREAKTHROUGH

You don't always realize God is guiding your steps—until you look back and see the footprints.

After everything my wife and I had endured—abuse, addiction, psychosis, and years of fighting to survive—I never imagined the next chapter of my healing would begin with a bad back and a work assignment I never asked for. But that's how God works. He doesn't always shout His plans; sometimes, He whispers them through pain.

In December of 2022, I suffered a serious back injury at work. I had dealt with physical pain before, but this was different. An MRI revealed what doctors described in medical terms, but all I knew was that I was broken. Words like *annular fissure*, *disc protrusion*, and *nerve impingement* filled the report. The worst part was a moderate disc protrusion at L4-L5, causing narrowing in my spine and pinching the right L5 nerve root. I was in bad shape—constant pain, limited movement, and forced out of the job I had been doing for years. I went from transporting millions of dollars daily in an armored truck to light duty in an unfamiliar world.

But here's the beauty of God: when life seemed to sideline me, He was setting the board for a divine move.

My modified duty assignment landed me in a church—of all places. I was assigned to work with a nonprofit helping kids in an after-school program. It felt strange, like a total mismatch for someone with my background, but I showed up. Quiet. Observant. Just doing my time.

But week after week, something shifted.

The staff there began opening up, and eventually, I found myself conversing with another man on light duty. He worked for the city's transportation service. As we talked, I mentioned that I had also driven buses for the city in the early 2000s. That sparked something in him. He began rattling off names, and to his surprise—and mine—I knew many of the people he mentioned. Then he pulled out his phone and showed me a photo of an older gentleman.

"Do you know who this is?" he asked. I looked at the photo and froze.

"Yeah," I said, my voice filled with disbelief. "That's Mr. Coleman—my old supervisor."

He smiled and said, "You know he's a pastor?" I

blinked. "A pastor? As in, *church* pastor?"

"Yep," he said. "He has a church in southeast Fresno. Services every Sunday at 10 AM."

That moment floored me. My past and my present collided in the most unexpected place. I asked for the name of the church and looked it up the moment I got home. That Sunday, my wife and I decided to attend.

When we walked into that church, I felt something I hadn't felt in decades—*peace*. I hadn't been to church regularly since I was a teenager. I'd gone a few times in my early twenties, but it never truly felt like home. But this... this was different. It was like I had stepped back into something my soul had always longed for.

That Sunday, Pastor Coleman delivered a sermon titled *"You Are the Result of a Family Member's Prayers."*

I was stunned. It felt like he was speaking directly to me. Like he knew every silent tear, every sleepless night, every prayer I had whispered in the dark. My wife and I sat there, eyes wide, hearts full. That message pierced deep, not with pain—but with clarity. It was like God was saying, *"This, is what all the detours were for."*

After service, I walked up to Pastor Coleman. The last time I saw him was back in 2009. It was now 2023. Not only did he remember me, but he lit up with joy. We embraced like old friends who had both made it through the storm. He invited me to breakfast a few weeks later, and that conversation sealed it—my wife and I had found our spiritual home.

We've been attending ever since.

I often think back to how strange it seemed—being injured, reassigned, and planted in a church to do work that had nothing to do with my career. **But God had a plan**. He was moving pieces the whole time. He knew what my heart needed before I even asked.

But isn't that just like Him?

God used a back injury to get me back into His house. He used light duty to illuminate a dark place in my spirit. He used a chance encounter to reconnect me with a man from my past who would become my spiritual shepherd. What looked like a setback was the beginning of my return—not just to church, but to God's presence, God's people, and God's purpose for my life.

I was coming home...

Not just to a building...

But to *belonging*...

To faith...

To a God who had never stopped pursuing me. Yes, the road was painful. But every step had a purpose.

Proving once again...

the **Master had been playing chess**— while I had been playing checkers.

CONCLUSION

If you've made it this far, then maybe, like me, you've spent part of your life asking...

Why?

Why does life hurt so much?

Why do bad things happen to good people?

Why doesn't God step in sooner—louder—clearer?

I asked those questions. From the corner of a bedroom where I sat in punishment.

From the silence of a mother's rejection. From the chaos of my wife's illness.

From the aftermath of my own failures and betrayals. But looking back now, I see what I couldn't see then:

God was never absent...

He was never late...

While I was playing checkers...He was playing chess.

The difference between the two isn't just strategy—it's **vision**.

Checkers reacts...

Chess anticipates...

Checkers looks one move ahead...

Chess sees the end from the beginning...

While I was trying to survive the subsequent beating, the next heartbreak, the next breakdown—God was preparing the win.

Every heartbreak was a move...

Every betrayal was a setup...

Every blessing, delay, and person He sent was part of His divine strategy. And the most incredible part?

He didn't need me to understand His plan for it to work.

He just needed me to trust Him.

When I was sitting in despair, thinking life was just about reacting to the moment, God was quietly and patiently crafting a masterpiece. My abuela was one of His first chess pieces, planted firmly in my life with unconditional love, resilience, and wisdom. Her legacy didn't just comfort me—it prepared me. It shaped me into a man capable of loving deeply even when life turned cruel.

Then came Crystal—a piece I once thought was just another chaotic part of my broken life. But now I know: she was God's most crucial move.

We were two shattered souls brought together not by chance but by divine design.

Her love pulled me from darkness when I was drowning in it. Her belief in me helped me see the man I could become. Her strength taught me that brokenness doesn't disqualify you. It's often the very thing God uses to rebuild you into someone new.

Crystal saw in me what I could not see in myself—and through her, God showed me a love that doesn't just heal wounds but rewrites destinies. When she told me to write my story, I dismissed her. I was still believing the old lies—the ones that said my voice and life didn't matter.

But God's plan never depended on my belief in myself. He had already planted the seed. It simply had to bloom in its season. And bloom it did—through long nights of caregiving, through hospitals and healing, through notebooks full of pain-turned-purpose.

Writing gave me my voice…

Speaking gave me my calling…

And through it all, I realized something I will carry until my last breath:

God never wastes pain.

He weaves it into purpose.

I once thought life was simple—a series of moves, good or bad, winning or losing.

But now I understand:

Life is not a game of checkers.

Life is a masterpiece of chess.

Every move is deliberate...

Every setback is strategic...

Every loss is pregnant with hidden victory...

And if you are standing somewhere in your own story—confused, broken, weary—I want you to know:

God is moving...

Even now...

Even here...

He's not reacting to your crisis. He's already woven it into your triumph. It won't always make sense. It won't always feel good. But it will always be **holy**.

You don't have to see every move. You just have to trust the One who already sees the **checkmate.**

My story isn't remarkable because I'm strong or wise or extraordinary...

It's remarkable because God is.

Because He is patient enough to work with broken pieces...

Strong enough to carry us through our darkest storms...

Faithful enough to finish the good work He started—even when we fight Him every step of the way. So let my life be a testimony to you:

God doesn't play games with our lives...

He plays with purpose...

And when it's His move, when the board looks the most chaotic, when it feels like all hope is lost—

That's when the King steps in... And He never loses.

www.ingramcontent.com/pod-product-compliance
Lightning Source LLC
Chambersburg PA
CBHW051236120626
46547CB00013B/1669